MONUMENTAL
VERSES

by J. Patrick Lewis

NATIONAL GEOGRAPHIC
WASHINGTON, D.C.

A bow to all who hoist the spirit high
And carve imagination into stone
By fire and forge, thrown hugely to the sky.
Whether they be well- or little-known,

The buildings in this picture book cement
A thought: No matter who the builders were,
They gave to time a timeless monument—
A human star-chitecture signature.

I cannot say what others make of this,
The mystery of Stonehenge, a Taj Mahal,
And yet I know how much the world would miss
Majesty at a glance if they should fall.

This book is for the curious at heart,
Startled at sights they seldom get to see
Or even dream of—science born of art,
Such works of genius these were meant to be.

TABLE OF CONTENTS

STONEHENGE

DATE: BUILT FROM 2800-1800 B.C.
LOCATION: SALISBURY PLAIN, WILTSHIRE, ENGLAND
BUILDER: THE BEAKER PEOPLE
PHYSICAL FACT: BLUESTONES AND SANDSTONES WERE HAULED IN FROM MARLBOROUGH DOWNS,
20 MILES (32 KM) AWAY. EVEN TODAY YOU CAN SEE THE DRAG MARKS.

Five thousand years ago, a star-struck night blinked down at them, huddled by twig fires among towering pines and hazel wood. Some spoke of weather, some of game, others told of death or heartbreak. Just as dawn sealed the envelope of night, someone uttered, for what was the first time in prehistory, a word for *monument*. A hush so deafening fell across that place that even tree moan and leaf fall stopped. Then, the earliest Timekeeper said, It must create shadows if Sun and Moon are to speak to us of their travels. Let stones be circular in praise, cried the first Priest, alive to prayer. Smooth out the chalk downland, said the first Henge-ineer. From the far north, drag giants of sandstone and bluestone to water, float them by raft, haul them over land. It will take us one hundred full moons to move a stone, the first Mathematician said. The Rope-weaver cautioned, We can expect no sympathy from the sea. Fifty generations from now, mused the old Philosopher, our ancestors might see it finally finished. Every one of the Beaker folk spoke in turn until only a small child was left to ask, How are you ever going to stand ten-ton stones upright? The wind carried away the answer before it was ever heard.

EASTER ISLAND

DATE: BUILT FROM A.D.1400 TO A.D.1600 A.D.
LOCATION: 2,300 MILES OFF THE COAST OF CHILE
BUILDER: INDIGENOUS PEOPLES
PHYSICAL FACT: THERE ARE NEARLY 900 GIANT STATUES ON THE ISLAND.

Volcanic ash carved into men,
Whose backs are turned against the sea—
The ancients show us now and then
A sense of mad nobility.

Dark heroes gazing at a sky
That never heeds our human cares
Are images that magnify
The possibilities of prayer,

Or high-flown hope, or an *homage*
Of people who cast their beliefs
Into this stone-faced entourage
Of big men, ancestors, and chiefs.

GREAT PYRAMID OF CHEOPS

DATE: BUILT 2589-2566 B.C.

LOCATION: GIZA, EGYPT

BUILDER: ESTIMATED 100,000 SLAVES

PHYSICAL FACT: 2,300,000 BLOCKS OF STONE, AVERAGE WEIGHT OF 2.5 TONS EACH

The
story of
this ancient
land, where wind's
a glove designing sand,
is told by ghosts in silent
rooms beneath the most enormous
tombs of granite fame. Some thirty years
the peasants came, gaunt brigadiers of stone
by rope. Without the wheel, their only
hope was grim ordeal. Where Pharaohs lie, a
Pyramid should glorify what others did.

GOLDEN GATE BRIDGE

DATE: BUILT 1933-1937
LOCATION: SAN FRANCISCO, CALIFORNIA
ARCHITECT: JOSEPH B. STRAUSS
PHYSICAL FACT: TOTAL LENGTH = 1.7 MILES

If I had to choose a
Nifty color
To cover a whole bridge with,
Especially one that
Reminded me of a sunset
Neighborhood in a sunshine country
And made people think, Oh
That's span-tastic, just right,
I wouldn't choose black and white
Or yellow stripes—
Not polka dots either!—
Although such colors do look
Lovely on zebras, tigers, and Dalmatians.

Once I had stirred ten truckloads of
Red raspberries, I'd
Add a couple of tons of squeezed California
Nectarines, and hefty barrels of golden
Grape juice in the sweetest coat that
Ever bedazzled a bridge over a bay.

ARC DE TRIOMPHE

DATE: BUILT 1806-1836
LOCATION: PARIS, FRANCE
BUILDERS: JEAN-FRANÇOIS-THÉRÈSE CHALGRIN AND JEAN-ARMAND RAYMOND
PHYSICAL FACT: 164 FT (50 M) HIGH AND 148 FT (45 M) WIDE

Triumphal Roman arcs
Were magic doors
For ancient soldiers who,
Surviving wars,
Resumed their lives
As ordinary men
By merely passing through
Them once again.

And now where these
Twelve avenues converge,
Napolean, DeGaulle,
And history merge
Into the Arc of what
We know as France—
Tradition, culture,
Paris, and romance.

ROSE CITY OF PETRA

DATE: MORE THAN 2,000 YEARS OLD
LOCATION: SOUTH JORDAN
BUILDER: NABATAEAN ARABS
PHYSICAL FACT: REDISCOVERED IN 1812 AFTER BEING "LOST" FOR THREE HUNDRED YEARS.

In pink and salmon-colored rock,
Arabs from a distant past
Carved what remains a future shock—

This city built of canyons lives
In mystic beauty, glory, and
Awe beyond superlatives.

Four hundred years the mountain home
Of traders who touched every land,
Petra, too soon sacked by Rome,

Is now a sandstone-rich archive
For climbers and the curious,
Like bees upon a honeyed hive.

No other cliffs, no canyon view
Recalls to mind or calls to man
Such genius as the world once knew.

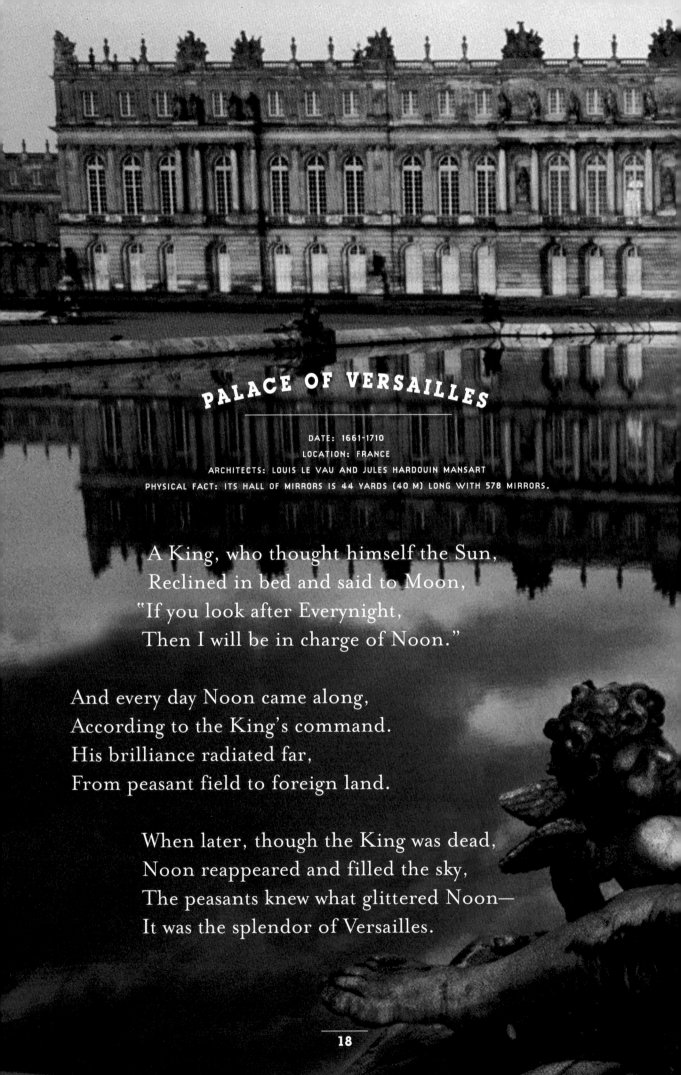

PALACE OF VERSAILLES

DATE: 1661-1710
LOCATION: FRANCE
ARCHITECTS: LOUIS LE VAU AND JULES HARDOUIN MANSART
PHYSICAL FACT: ITS HALL OF MIRRORS IS 44 YARDS (40 M) LONG WITH 578 MIRRORS.

A King, who thought himself the Sun,
Reclined in bed and said to Moon,
"If you look after Everynight,
Then I will be in charge of Noon."

And every day Noon came along,
According to the King's command.
His brilliance radiated far,
From peasant field to foreign land.

When later, though the King was dead,
Noon reappeared and filled the sky,
The peasants knew what glittered Noon—
It was the splendor of Versailles.

STATUE OF LIBERTY

DATE: ARRIVED FROM FRANCE ON JULY 4, 1884
LOCATION: NEW YORK, NEW YORK
ARCHITECT: FRÉDÉRIC AUGUSTE BARTHOLDI
PHYSICAL FACT: THE FOUNDATION ALONE REQUIRED 24,000 TONS OF CONCRETE.
IT TOOK SIX MONTHS TO MOUNT THE STATUE TO HER BASE.

My nose is four and a half feet long,
My mouth is three feet wide,
My head's ten feet from ear to ear...
I'm a gal you can step inside.

My hand is over sixteen feet,
I'm the first stop on the tour.
My index finger's eight feet long.
I'm America's signature.

My waist is thirty-five feet thick.
In tons, I'm two twenty-five—
I'm the biggest lady ever known
To keep freedom alive.

MACHU PICCHU

DATE: BUILT A.D.1460-1470
LOCATION: PERU
BUILDER: THE INCA
PHYSICAL FACT: AT AN ALTITUDE OF 8,000 FEET (2400 M), THIS REALM
WAS FORGOTTEN AFTER THE INCA DIED OF SMALLPOX AND WAS
REDISCOVERED IN 1911 BY A YALE PROFESSOR.

Above the raintree country of their birth,
In ancient days the Inca hid from earth
A testament—"Old Peak"—in massive stone,
A secret sacred city all their own,
Invisible to enemies below.
   That sky, abandoned centuries ago,
      Where people gazed at each celestial gem
         As if the teeming stars were watching them,
            Remains as green and veiled a mist-ery
               As humankind is privileged to see.

THE EIFFEL TOWER

DATE: BUILT 1887-1889
LOCATION: PARIS, FRANCE
ARCHITECT: GUSTAVE EIFFEL
PHYSICAL FACT: THE PANORAMIC VIEW FROM THE TOP IS BEST ONE HOUR BEFORE SUNSET.

Three hundred workers nailed you,
The Prince of Wales unveiled you.
Your countrymen have hailed you a star.

A mountaineer has scaled you,
Two parachutists sailed you,
A million postcards mailed you afar.

Gustave Eiffel intended you
To be so sleek and splendid, you
Know nothing has transcended you, *mon cher.*

We tourists recommended you,
Ascended and descended you,
And all of us befriended you...up there!

MOUNT RUSHMORE

DATE: BUILT 1927-1941
LOCATION: SOUTH DAKOTA, USA
CHIEF ENGINEER: GUTZON BORGLUM
PHYSICAL FACT: BORGLUM WAS ONE OF AMERICA'S MOST SUCCESSFUL PAINTERS
LONG BEFORE HE EVEN CONSIDERED MOUNT RUSHMORE.

Gutzon Borglum designed four faces
that trumpeted American history
across the western skyline.
Four hundred miners built roads,
blasted stone, sharpened drill bits,
ran the hoists and generated power.

Norman "Happy" Anderson, a skilled
powderman, earned $1.25 an hour,
more than mines were paying at the time.
Describing his presidential task, Happy's
dynamite words were worthy of a bonus:

I put the curl in Lincoln's beard,
the part in Teddy's hair,
and the twinkle in Washington's eye.

GREAT WALL OF CHINA

DATE: BUILT FROM 3RD CENTURY B.C. TO 20TH CENTURY A.D.
LOCATION: JINSHANLING, CHINA
BUILDER: ABOUT HALF A MILLION PEOPLE
PHYSICAL FACT: 1,500 MILES LONG (2,400 KM)

This
fabled
monument
of earth
and brick
and stone,
designed
by nothing
more than
bucket,
cup, and
spoon,
is still
the
only
structure
built
by human
hands
some
thought
you'd
see if
you
were
standing
on the
moon.

EPILOGUE

If, as the poet Dante Gabriel Rossetti once wrote, a poem is a "moment's monument," then perhaps a monument is a timeless poem. When I first thought about honoring some of the world's enduring man-made constructions, I was humbled by wonder, subdued by such towering greatness.

How to begin? Once I overcame awe, the difficult task of selection arose. It will be obvious to any reader that the subjects in this book are only a few of the finest architectural achievements of humankind. If your favorite is missing—the Leaning Tower of Pisa, the Taj Mahal, Japan's Imperial Palace?—I invite you to write a poem about it.

Try any poetic form that appeals to you: free verse, ballad, acrostic, shaped poem. I tried to make the form match the building itself in some small, indirect way that spoke to me. Pretend your pen is a camera: Take a picture of the monument, but only with your words. And who knows? The word picture you capture may turn out to be as captivating and satisfying as the the image that inspired you.

JPL

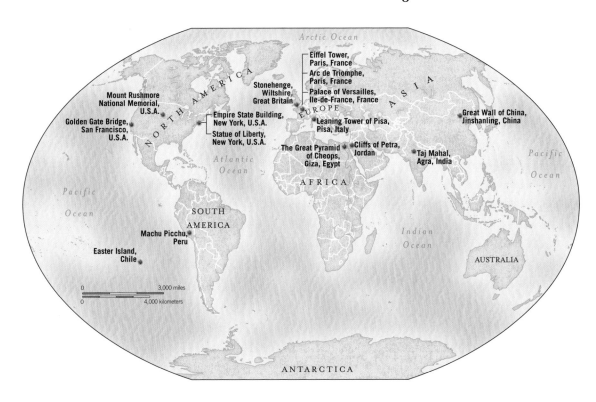

EIFFEL TOWER
PARIS, FRANCE
(COVER) The City of Paris owns this 10,100 ton structure. Six million visitors annually travel up its 1,665 steps and nine elevators to reach the top. The elevators travel the equivalent of two and half times around the world each year. DALLAS AND JOHN HEATON/CORBIS

TAJ MAHAL
AGRA, UTTAR PRADESH, INDIA
(TITLE PAGE) In 1630 the Emperor Shah Jehan lost his wife as she gave birth to their 14th child. The Taj Mahal, her tomb, took 23 years to build. It is covered in white marble and surrounded by four minarets. GEORGINA BOWATER/CORBIS

STONEHENGE
WILTSHIRE, ENGLAND
Speculation on the reasons Stonehenge was built range from human sacrifice to astronomy. It seems to have been designed to allow for observation of astronomical phenomena—summer and winter solstices, eclipses, and more. DAVID PATERSON/GETTY IMAGES

EASTER ISLAND
EASTER ISLAND, CHILE
No written record remains of those who built nearly 900 giant stone "maoi" averaging 13 feet (4m) and 14 tons each, but they might represent the spirits of famous ancestors—or simply the human imagination set in stone. THOMAS HOEPKER/MAGNUM.

GOLDEN GATE BRIDGE
SAN FRANCISCO, CALIFORNIA
Rumor has it that the U.S. Navy wanted to paint the Golden Gate Bridge black with yellow stripes to make it more visible to passing ships. Architects chose international orange to blend with California's beauty and natural surroundings. ROGER RESSMEYER/CORBIS

GREAT PYRAMID OF CHEOPS
GIZA, EGYPT
Many have guessed how the Great Pyramid was built; none have provided a definitive answer. Not much is known about the pharaoh Cheops. His tomb had been robbed long before archaeologists came upon it. LARRY LEE/CORBIS

EMPIRE STATE BUILDING
MANHATTAN, NEW YORK
How many millions of Earth's tourists have visited the 86th and 102nd floor observatories of the Empire State Building? Constructed in just one year and 45 days, this legendary structure opened on May 1, 1931. ALAN SCHEIN/CORBIS

ARC DE TRIOMPHE
PARIS, FRANCE
This famous structure, the largest triumphal arch in the world, was begun in 1806 at the whim of Napoleon Bonaparte to glorify himself, his army, and his military victories. Beneath this national war memorial lies the tomb of the unknown soldier. DAVID HIGGS/CORBIS

ROSE CITY OF PETRA
PETRA, TURKEY
The very success of Petra as a caravan crosssroads attracted the attention of the Roman Empire, which annexed it. Its glory waned, and the sandstone cliff paradise fell into disuse, to be "rediscovered" by a Swiss adventurer in 1812. ANDY CHADWICK/GETTY IMAGES

PALACE OF VERSAILLES
ILE-DE-FRANCE, FRANCE
In 1668 France's Louis the 14th, who thought himself divine, decided to build a palace outside Paris away from the boisterous crowds but close to prime hunting grounds. The French Revolution of 1789 deposed King Louis the 16th. BRUNO BARBEY, MAGNUM

STATUE OF LIBERTY
LIBERTY ISLAND, NEW YORK HARBOR
One hundred years after America's War of Independence, which the French did so much to help win, France presented the U.S. with a lasting monument to commemorate the two countries' abiding friendship and love of freedom. CORBIS

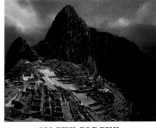

MACHU PICCHU
MACHU PICCHU, PERU
Most likely a religious retreat or royal estate, Machu Picchu was known to few people, even among the Inca. When Pizarro and the Spanish conquistadors arrived, much of the Inca population had died of smallpox. It was rediscoved in 1911. ED FREEMAN/GETTY IMAGES

THE EIFFEL TOWER
PARIS, FRANCE
The Eiffel Tower was built to honor the 100th anniversary of the French Revolution. Among its statistics: 40 tons of paint, 1,652 steps to the top, and a sway of up to 4.8 inches (12 cm) in high winds. REUTERS/CORBIS

MOUNT RUSHMORE
MOUNT RUSHMORE NATIONAL MEMORIAL, SOUTH DAKOTA
Between 1927 and 1941, Gutzon Borglum and his team chiseled those four famous presidential faces by removing some 450,000 tons of granite, most of it with dynamite. CORBIS

GREAT WALL OF CHINA
JINSHANLING, CHINA
Astronauts assure us that the Great Wall cannot be seen from the moon: nothing man-made can. The Great Wall of China is not continuous. It is a collection of short walls that often follow the crest of hills on the southern edge of the Mongolian plain. LIU LIQUN/CORBIS

LEANING TOWER OF PISA
TUSCANY REGION, ITALY
(BACK COVER) This circular bell tower began its famous lean during construction. After extensive studies of the plans and testing of the subsoil, the cause of the lean is still a mystery. O. LOUIS MAZZATENTA / NG IMAGE COLLECTION

FOR LEE BENNETT HOPKINS, GRAMMAGABOODLE
ANTHOLOGIST AND SWELLIFFILASTICAL FRIEND
JPL

———————————————

Published by the National Geographic Society.

Book Designers: Bea Jackson and David M. Seager
Illustrations Editor: Janet Dustin
Titles in this book are set in ITC Lubalin Bold.
The text is set in Mrs. Eaves and captions are set in Citizen, both fonts by Emigre.

Library of Congress Cataloging-in-Publication Information is available
from the Library of Congress upon request.

Trade Edition ISBN 0-7922-7135-1   Library Edition ISBN 0-7922-7139-4

The world's largest nonprofit scientific and educational organization,
the National Geographic Society was founded in 1888
"for the increase and diffusion of geographic knowledge."
Since then it has supported scientific exploration and spread information
to its more than eight million members worldwide.

The National Geographic Society educates and inspires millions every day through magazines, books,
television programs, videos, maps and atlases, research grants, the National Geographic Bee, teacher
workshops, and innovative classroom materials. The Society is supported through membership dues,
charitable gifts, and income from the sale of its educational products. Members receive
NATIONAL GEOGRAPHIC magazine—the Society's official journal—discounts on Society products
and other benefits. For more information about the National Geographic Society,
its educational programs and publications, and ways to support its work,
please call 1-800-NGS-LINE (647-5463) or write to the following address:

NATIONAL GEOGRAPHIC SOCIETY
1145 17th Street N.W.
Washington, D.C. 20036-4688 U.S.A.
Visit the Society's Web site: www.nationalgeographic.com

PRINTED IN BELGIUM